BIGGEST NAMES IN MUSIC

ED SHEERAN

by Emma Huddleston

FOCUS READERS

NAVIGATOR

WWW.FOCUSREADERS.COM

Focus Readers is distributed by North Star Editions:
sales@northstareditions.com | 888-417-0195

Produced for Focus Readers by Red Line Editorial.

Photographs ©: Charles Sykes/Invision/AP Images, cover, 1; Ivan Vodop'janov/Kommersant/Sipa USA/AP Images, 4–5; Shutterstock Images, 7, 12, 20–21, 29; Stuart Hogben/Retna/Photoshot/Newscom, 8–9; SI1/WENN/Newscom, 11; Jonathan Short/Invision/AP Images, 14–15; JMAB/VMAB/WENN/Newscom, 17; John Marshall/AP Images, 18; Matt Sayles/Invision/AP Images, 23; Joel C. Ryan/Invision/AP Images, 24; Yui Mok/PA Wire URN:19382724/Press Association/AP Images, 27

Library of Congress Cataloging-in-Publication Data
Names: Huddleston, Emma, author.
Title: Ed Sheeran / by Emma Huddleston.
Description: Lake Elmo, MN : Focus Readers, 2021. | Series: Biggest names in music | Includes index. | Audience: Grades 4-6
Identifiers: LCCN 2020011130 (print) | LCCN 2020011131 (ebook) | ISBN 9781644936382 (hardcover) | ISBN 9781644936474 (paperback) | ISBN 9781644936658 (pdf) | ISBN 9781644936566 (ebook)
Subjects: LCSH: Sheeran, Ed, 1991---Juvenile literature. | Singers--England--Biography--Juvenile literature.
Classification: LCC ML3930.S484 H84 2021 (print) | LCC ML3930.S484 (ebook) | DDC 782.42164092 [B]--dc23
LC record available at https://lccn.loc.gov/2020011130
LC ebook record available at https://lccn.loc.gov/2020011131

Printed in the United States of America
Mankato, MN
082020

ABOUT THE AUTHOR

Emma Huddleston lives in the Twin Cities with her husband. She enjoys writing children's books and staying active. She thinks music is an important part of life and spends some afternoons learning how to play the piano.

TABLE OF CONTENTS

CHAPTER 1

ARTIST OF THE DECADE

Ed Sheeran's concert in Moscow, Russia, was about to begin. The crowd clapped and cheered. But the stage was empty. Instead, huge screens showed Sheeran walking backstage. The British singer wore a black T-shirt and jeans. His red hair was easy to spot in the dark hallways.

Ed Sheeran performs at the Otkritie Arena in Moscow, Russia, in July 2019.

Sheeran smiled as he neared the stage. Then he grabbed his guitar and started strumming. Fans immediately recognized his hit song "Castle on the Hill." They sang along as lights flashed on the screens. Some fans took videos on their smartphones. Others danced or pumped their fists.

The concert was part of Sheeran's tour for his new album. It was one of the biggest tours in history. Sheeran played 255 shows in 43 countries. The shows sold nearly nine million tickets.

Sheeran's path to success had not been easy. But he had become a worldwide star. In December 2019, Sheeran was

Sheeran played at the Stade de France in 2018. This huge stadium holds more than 80,000 people.

named the UK Artist of the Decade for 2010–2019. During those years, Sheeran had 12 **singles** or albums that reached No. 1. That was more than any other artist in the United Kingdom.

CHAPTER 2

FOLLOWING HIS DREAM

Edward Christopher Sheeran was born on February 17, 1991. He grew up in Framlingham, a town in Suffolk, England. Ed loved music from a young age. At age four, he was part of a church choir. He started playing guitar a few years later. Ed had natural talent. And his parents, John and Imogen, encouraged him.

Ed returned to Suffolk to perform in the Latitude Festival in 2011.

Ed began writing music when he was 11. Soon, he was recording his songs. By 2005, he had made two **EPs**. He called them *Spinning Man* and *The Orange Room*. Ed even played some small shows.

Before he finished high school, Ed left home and moved to London, England. He brought his guitar and a backpack stuffed

SPEAKING THROUGH MUSIC

Ed was bullied at school. Kids made fun of his red hair and glasses. They also made fun of the way he talked. Ed had a stutter. Speaking in class was hard for him. But rapping helped. Ed learned all the words to his favorite rap songs. Practicing the fast lyrics helped him eventually get over his stutter.

Early in his career, Ed often played at small venues, such as cafés and music stores.

with clothes. He hoped his music career would take off.

But life in the big city wasn't easy. Ed was just a teenager. He often played music as a busker. Buskers perform in public places such as streets or parks.

Fans enjoy seeing how the images in Ed's music videos add to the songs.

Most are not paid to play. Instead, they ask listeners for donations of money.

Sometimes Ed didn't make enough money for food. He slept in parks or on subway trains. At times, he was close to giving up and going back home. But his passion for music kept him going.

Ed kept recording music and playing at local events. He released two more EPs in 2006 and 2007. And in 2009, he performed in more than 300 live shows.

In 2010, Ed started posting videos of his music online. The videos had viewers from all around the world. One was the rapper Example, who invited Ed to be the **opener** for his tour.

Ed was proud of how far he had come. But he wanted to keep building his career. To do that, he felt he needed to move again. This time, he would go all the way to the United States.

CHAPTER 3

SIGNING A RECORD DEAL

In 2010, Sheeran moved to Los Angeles, California. He didn't have a place to live. But he was determined to follow his dream. Sheeran sent some of his songs to people who worked in the music business. Sheeran hoped they would offer him a **record deal**. But he did not receive any responses.

In his music, Sheeran often alternates between singing and rapping.

One day in late 2010, Sheeran had the opportunity to perform live on a local radio show. The show's host was Jamie Foxx. Foxx was a singer and **producer**. He thought Sheeran had talent. Foxx offered to let Sheeran sleep on his couch and use his recording studio for a short time.

Sheeran released another EP in January 2011. Listeners loved it. It reached the No. 2 spot on iTunes. At the time, iTunes was the most popular place to get music online. The EP's success gave Sheeran the boost he needed. He signed with Atlantic Records by the end of the month.

Sheeran's first full-length album was released in September. It was a big hit.

"The A Team" was the first single Sheeran released with Atlantic Records.

Within six months, it sold more than one million copies. And in 2012, Sheeran won British Male Solo Artist and British Breakthrough Act at the BRIT Awards.

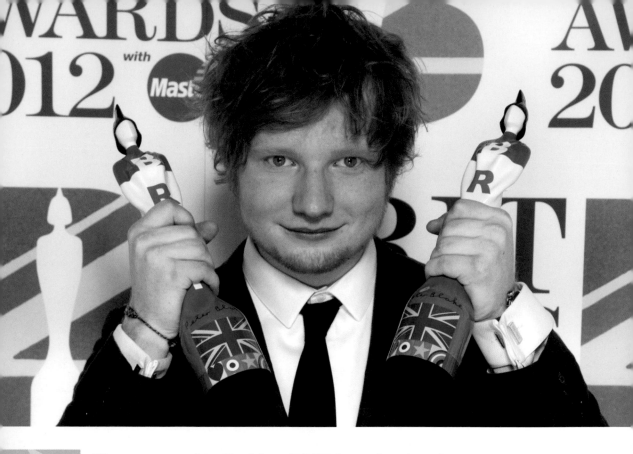

Sheeran won his first two BRIT Awards when he was just 21 years old.

Sheeran began gaining attention from people around the world. His single "The A Team" became a Top 10 song in Australia, Japan, Norway, and New Zealand. It also earned Sheeran his first Grammy Award **nomination**.

Sheeran's second album came out in June 2014. It was No. 1 in the United States and the United Kingdom. Three of the album's songs were ranked in the Top 10 on *Billboard*'s Hot 100. One was "Thinking Out Loud." This song won two Grammy Awards in 2016.

SONGWRITING STYLE

Many of Sheeran's hit songs are ballads. Ballads have a slow, smooth sound. But Sheeran's music includes rap and pop beats as well. Sheeran is also known for his songwriting. His songs often tell stories. Others express his feelings. He tries to write songs that are true and honest. Fans can connect with the emotional lyrics.

CHAPTER 4

WORLDWIDE STAR

In 2016, Sheeran slowed his pace. He took a break from touring and gave few performances. He focused on making his third album. Two singles from this album came out in January 2017. They were "Shape of You" and "Castle on the Hill." Fans loved them. Both songs reached the Top 10 on *Billboard*'s Hot 100.

Sheeran often writes songs based on experiences in his life.

"Shape of You" even topped the chart for several weeks.

When the new album came out in March 2017, fans rushed to hear it. In fact, Sheeran broke a record on the **streaming** platform Spotify. In 24 hours, his album had more than 56 million listens. The album also earned Sheeran two more Grammy Awards. It was named Best Pop Vocal Album, and "Shape of You" won Best Pop Solo Performance.

In February 2018, Sheeran won the BRIT Award for Global Success. He sang "Supermarket Flowers" at the awards ceremony. This song was about Sheeran's grandmother. She had passed away while

Sheeran performs "Shape of You" at the 59th Grammys.

he was making the album. Sheeran gave a quiet performance. A spotlight shone on the microphone where he stood. The rest of the stage lights stayed low. A piano and guitar played softly behind him.

Fans wave their phones as Sheeran sings during the 2018 BRIT Awards.

The audience swayed back and forth as Sheeran sang. Some people cried.

Throughout 2018, Sheeran recorded songs with many different music artists. *No. 6 Collaborations Project* came out in

August 2019. The album had 15 songs. For each song, Sheeran worked with a different artist or group.

The songs showed Sheeran's range of talent and wide popularity. He could sing many styles of music. And he could please fans of many **genres** and artists.

PRIVATE LIFE

Sheeran tends to keep details of his personal life separate from his fame as a singer. For example, he waited a while before talking about his marriage to Cherry Seaborn. They first met in high school in England. Then they moved to the United States at different times and for different reasons. Later, the two met again and fell in love. In December 2018, they had a small, secret wedding in their home.

Critics were impressed as well. The album earned a Grammy nomination for Best Pop Vocal Album.

Beyond music, Sheeran has supported many causes. He has helped raise money at events focused on AIDS and poverty. In 2019, he donated more than 300 items to a **charity** in England. He gave clothes, stuffed animals, toys, CDs, and more.

Sheeran supports youth organizations, too. In December 2019, he launched the Ed Sheeran Suffolk Music Foundation. Sheeran wanted to give back to the area where he grew up. So, his charity gives money to young musicians who live in Suffolk, England. The musicians must

Sheeran performs with Mike Rosenberg at a charity concert for the Teenage Cancer Trust.

be under 18 years old. They can use the money to buy instruments, take music classes, or help get their careers started. In this way, Sheeran hopes to encourage other young people to keep following their dreams, just like he did.

ED SHEERAN

- Birth date: February 17, 1991
- Birthplace: Halifax, West Yorkshire, England
- Family members: Imogen (mother), John (father), Matthew (brother)
- High school: Thomas Mills High School
- Major accomplishments:
  - January 2011: Sheeran signs with Atlantic Records.
  - February 2012: Sheeran wins BRIT Awards for British Male Solo Artist and British Breakthrough Act.
  - February 2016: "Thinking Out Loud" wins two Grammys.
  - February 2018: Sheeran wins the BRIT Award for Global Success.
  - December 2019: Sheeran is named the UK Artist of the Decade for 2010–2019.

Sheeran performs in the Czech Republic in 2015.

- Quote: "The more you write tunes, the better they will become. The more you do gigs, the better you will become. It's just kind of like the facts of life; the 'practice makes perfect' thing. Keep your fingers crossed, start from the bottom, and work your way up."

Ilana Kaplan. "Redhead Redemption: Ed Sheeran." *Interview*. Interview Magazine, 14 Dec. 2011. Web. 25 Feb. 2020.

FOCUS ON
ED SHEERAN

Write your answers on a separate piece of paper.

1. Write a paragraph summarizing the main ideas of Chapter 2.

2. If you were famous, would you share many details about your private life with your fans? Why or why not?

3. On which album did Sheeran record songs with many different artists?
   - **A.** *Spinning Man*
   - **B.** *The Orange Room*
   - **C.** *No. 6 Collaborations Project*

4. Why would a record deal be helpful for a musician?
   - **A.** Writing songs is impossible without a record deal.
   - **B.** The record company would help musicians record and sell their songs.
   - **C.** The record company would let musicians post their music online.

Answer key on page 32.

GLOSSARY

charity
An organization set up to help people in need.

EPs
Collections of several songs, often with half the number of songs on full-length albums.

genres
Categories of music, such as rock, pop, or country.

nomination
When a person, song, or album is chosen as a finalist for an award or honor.

opener
A group or performer that plays before the main act.

producer
A person who works with musicians to record songs.

record deal
An agreement where an artist makes an album that a company sells and promotes.

singles
Songs that are released on their own.

streaming
Playing videos or music by sending information over the internet.

TO LEARN MORE

BOOKS

Boone, Mary. *Behind-the-Scenes Music Careers*. North Mankato, MN: Capstone Press, 2017.

Gagne, Tammy. *Ed Sheeran*. Hallandale, FL: Mitchell Lane Publishers, 2018.

Seigel, Rachel. *Ed Sheeran*. New York: Crabtree Publishing Company, 2018.

NOTE TO EDUCATORS

Visit **www.focusreaders.com** to find lesson plans, activities, links, and other resources related to this title.

INDEX

Answer Key: **1.** Answers will vary; **2.** Answers will vary; **3.** C; **4.** B